ANIMALS

eXtreme FACTS

BY STEFFI CAVELL-CLARKE

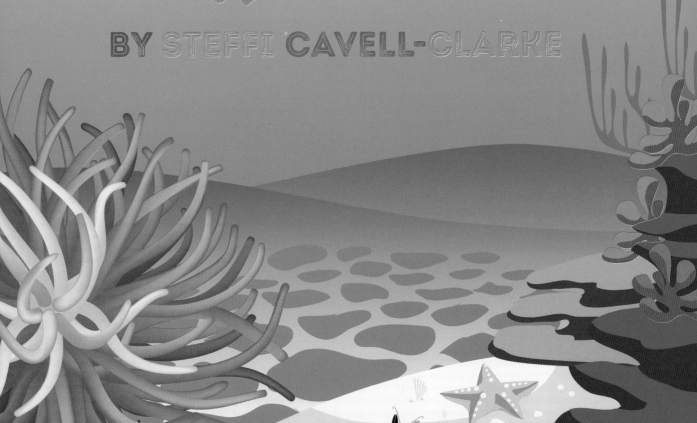

©2019
The Secret Book
Company
King's Lynn
Norfolk PE30 4LS

ISBN: 978-1-912502-37-0

Written by:
Steffi Cavell-Clarke
Edited by:
Kirsty Holmes
Designed by:
Jasmine Pointer

A catalogue record for this book
is available from the British Library.

PHOTO CREDITS

Abbreviations: l-left, r-right, b-bottom, t-top, c-centre, m-middle.

CONTENTS

Words that look like <u>this</u> can be found in the glossary on page 24.

ANIMALS

Animals are living things. Most animals need food, water and oxygen, and can <u>reproduce</u>. Studying animals is called zoology.

Animals live all over planet Earth. There are many different <u>species</u> and they come in many different shapes and sizes.

The animal kingdom includes over eight million known living species, but there are still nearly 10,000 new species of animal discovered every year.

Even though every species of animal is unique, they still share certain <u>traits</u>. We use these traits to group animals together. There are six main groups of animal.

Mammals

Birds

Fish

Reptiles

Amphibians

Invertebrates

Even though they may look different, many animals share similar body parts, such as eyes, ears and mouths. Let's take a closer look!

MAMMALS

A mammal is a type of animal that breathes air using <u>lungs</u>, has a backbone and usually grows hair on its body.

Polar bears live in the freezing Arctic.

Camels live in hot deserts.

Most mammals give birth to live <u>young</u> and produce milk to feed them.

Bats live in dark caves and can fly.

Dolphins live and swim in the oceans.

Human beings are mammals too. There are over 7 billion humans on Earth!

There are over 4,000 different types of mammal, and they all do weird and wonderful things!

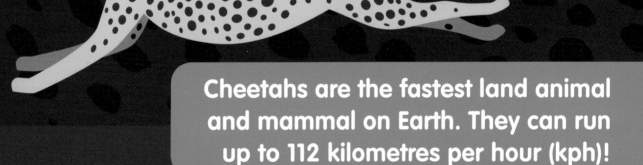

The largest mammal on the planet is the blue whale. The blue whale can grow up to 30 metres (m) long and weigh up to 180 tonnes!

Cheetahs are the fastest land animal and mammal on Earth. They can run up to 112 kilometres per hour (kph)!

Lots of mammals have tails. Cats and kangaroos use their tails for balance. Dogs wag their tails when they are happy.

BIRDS

A bird is a type of animal which lays eggs, and has a backbone, feathers and a hard beak.

All birds have wings and most birds use them to fly, but there are some <u>flightless</u> birds too, such as ostriches and penguins.

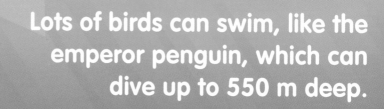

Lots of birds can swim, like the emperor penguin, which can dive up to 550 m deep.

All birds have hard beaks which help them to catch and eat their <u>prey</u>.

The smallest bird on Earth is the bee hummingbird, which measures around five centimetres (cm).

The largest bird on Earth is the ostrich, which stands at around 2.7 m tall.

Many species of birds build homes out of <u>materials</u> that blend in with their surroundings.

Birds build nests so that they have a safe place to lay their eggs and raise their young.

FISH

A fish is a type of cold-blooded animal that has a backbone, gills, fins and a <u>streamlined</u> body covered in scales.

Fins

Gills

Scales

All fish have gills and fins which allow them to breathe and swim underwater.

Sharks, rays, eels and salmon are all types of fish.

There are over 30,000 known species of fish alive today. All fish must live in water to survive.

The largest species of fish on Earth is the whale shark, which can grow up to 19 m long.

The great white shark **has very powerful** senses that can detect movements in the water: even fish lying under **the sand!**

Dolphins and whales breathe using two lungs, which means that they are mammals, not fish!

REPTILES

There are over 9,000 species of reptile in the world today.

Reptiles have backbones and their skin is almost completely covered in scales.

Reptiles usually live on land but some, such as turtles and crocodiles, can also live in water.

Reptiles are cold-blooded animals, which means that their body temperature matches their surrounding environment.

Tortoises and turtles are reptiles that have bony shells on their backs, which they can hide in when they sense danger.

The Galapágos tortoise is the largest tortoise on the planet. They can grow up to 1.5 m long and can live for up to 175 years!

Crocodiles and alligators are large reptiles with very powerful jaws and tails.

AMPHIBIANS

An amphibian is a type of cold-blooded animal that lays eggs and has a backbone.

Salamanders, newts and frogs are all types of amphibian.

Amphibians can live in water and on land. This is called being 'amphibious'.

Amphibians have a thin layer of slime that covers their

LIFE CYCLE OF A FROG

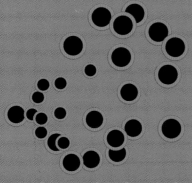

1) A female frog lays her eggs in fresh water.

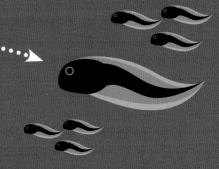

2) A tadpole wriggles out of each egg.

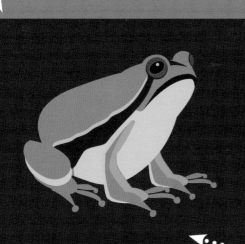

4) The froglets grow into adult frogs.

3) The tadpoles changes into froglets.

INVERTEBRATES

Invertebrates are animals that do not have a backbone. They can be small, like an insect, or huge, like a giant squid.

Some have soft bodies, such as worms, slugs and jellyfish.

Other invertebrates, such as insects and spiders, have a hard outer body called an exoskeleton. This protects their body like a suit of armour.

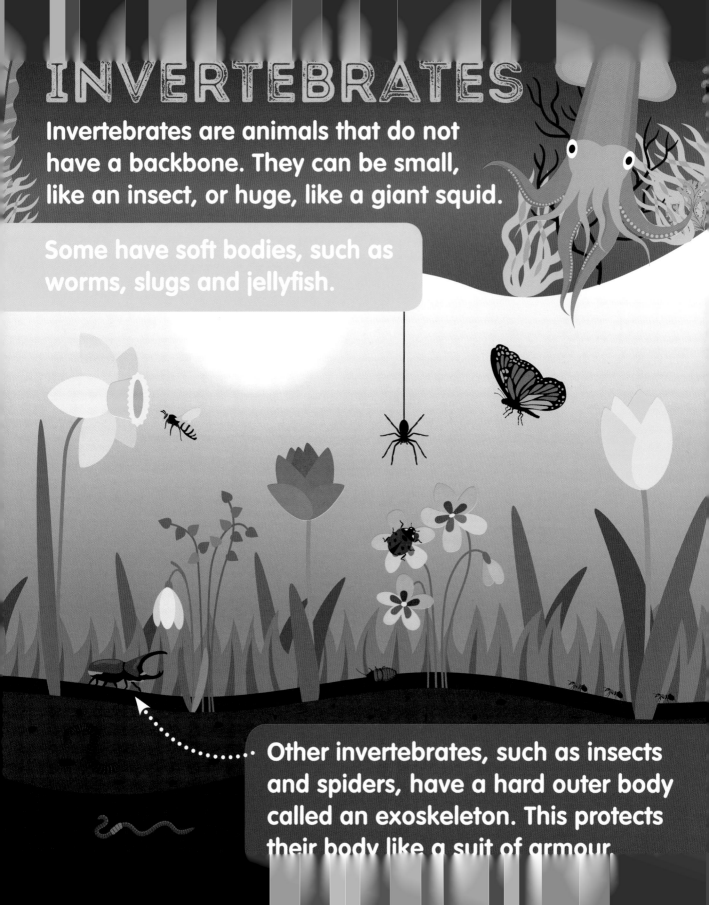

Thorax

Head

Abdomen

Insects have **three** main body parts. These are called the head, thorax and abdomen.

Over 96% of all the animal species on Earth are invertebrates.

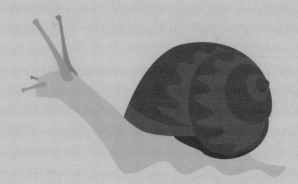

Some invertebrates have **shells** that help to protect them from predators.

ADAPTATION

Adaptation is a process that living things go through in order to fit in with their environment. For example, polar bears have adapted to have thick, heavy coats to keep them warm in cold climates.

The animals that have adapted to their environments are much more likely to survive than those who haven't.

Adaptation can take a very long time. It can change how an animal looks, how they behave and how easily they can reproduce.

Adaptation has led to millions of different animals that can survive in different types of habitat.

Camels have adapted to have large, flat feet so they can easily walk on sand, and long thick eyelashes to keep sand out of their eyes.

Many animals have adapted to <u>migrate</u> to warmer climates when their environments get too cold during the winter.

Giraffes have adapted to have long necks so they can reach the leaves on tall trees.

HABITATS

A habitat is a place where an animal lives. It can provide an animal with food, water and shelter. There are many different types of habitat around the world.

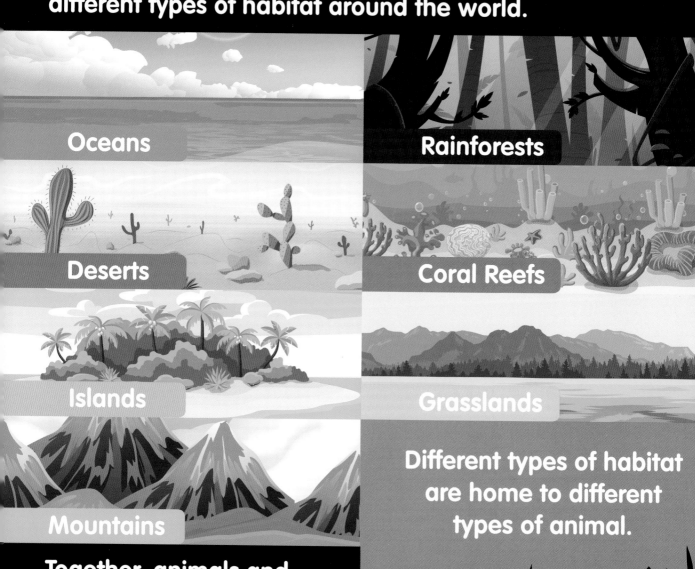

Oceans

Rainforests

Deserts

Coral Reefs

Islands

Grasslands

Mountains

Different types of habitat are home to different types of animal.

Together, animals and their habitats help to keep the environment healthy.

An ocean habitat is a very large area of salty seawater. It covers around 71% of the Earth's surface. That's a big home for lots of different animals!

A desert is a large area of land that receives very little rainfall. It can be a very harsh environment, but many animals have adapted to survive there.

Rainforests are forests that often experience heavy rainfall. From the treetops to the forest floor, rainforests are full of animal life.

EXTREME ANIMAL FACTS

The bat is the only mammal that can fly.

A tarantula spider can survive for more than two years without food.

Flamingos can only eat when their heads are upside down!

No tigers have the same stripes. Each tiger is different.

Alligators cannot move backwards.

The starfish is the only animal that can turn its stomach inside-out.

The ocean sunfish lays around **300** million eggs at one time; that's more **than any other animal!**

Frogs do not drink water; they absorb it through their skin instead.

An ant can carry up to **50 times** its own body **weight.**

Ostriches lay the **biggest** eggs in the world.

Sheep have **four** stomachs!

GLOSSARY

environment   the surrounding area

flightless   cannot fly

lungs   organs that animals use to breathe air

materials   what something is made of

migrate   move from one place to another based on seasonal changes

predators   animals that hunt other animals for food

prey   animals that are hunted by other animals for food

reproduce   to produce young through the act of mating

species   a group of very similar animals that are capable of producing young together

streamlined   something that is shaped to have low resistance in water and air

traits   qualities or characteristics

young   an animal's offspring

INDEX